SIDNEY CROSBY

VS.

WAYNE GRETZKY

BY WILL GRAVES

SportsZone

An Imprint of Abdo Publishing
abdopublishing.com

abdopublishing.com

Published by Abdo Publishing, a division of ABDO, PO Box 398166, Minneapolis,
Minnesota 55439. Copyright © 2018 by Abdo Consulting Group, Inc. International
copyrights reserved in all countries. No part of this book may be reproduced in any form
without written permission from the publisher. SportsZone™ is a trademark and logo of
Abdo Publishing.

Printed in the United States of America, North Mankato, Minnesota
102017
012018

Cover Photos: Julian Avram/Icon Sportswire/AP Images, left; B. Bennett/Bruce Bennett/
Getty Images, right
Interior Photos: Bruce Bennett Studios/Bruce Bennett/Getty Images, 4–5; Frank
Franklin II/AP Images, 5; Paul Kennedy/Sports Illustrated/Getty Images, 6–7; Ron Frehm/
AP Images, 8; Chris O'Meara/AP Images, 10; B. Bennett/Bruce Bennett/Getty Images,
12–13, 18–19; Bettmann/Getty Images, 14; Jeanine Leech/Icon Sportswire/AP Images,
15, 16; Manny Millan/Sports Illustrated/Getty Images, 20; Gene Puskar/AP Images, 22; Jim
McIsaac/Getty Images Sport/Getty Images, 24–25; Gene J. Puskar/AP Images, 26; Rusty
Kennedy/AP Images, 28

Editor: Patrick Donnelly
Series Designer: Sarah Winkler

Publisher's Cataloging-in-Publication Data
Names: Graves, Will, author.
Title: Sidney Crosby vs. Wayne Gretzky / by Will Graves.
Other titles: Sidney Crosby versus Wayne Gretzky
Description: Minneapolis, Minnesota : Abdo Publishing, 2018. | Series: Versus | Includes
    online resources and index.
Identifiers: LCCN 2017946928 | ISBN 9781532113581 (lib.bdg.) | ISBN 9781532152467
    (ebook)
Subjects: LCSH: Hockey players--Juvenile literature. | Hockey--Records--Juvenile
    literature. | Sports--History--Juvenile literature.
Classification: DDC 796.962--dc23
LC record available at https://lccn.loc.gov/2017946928

TABLE OF CONTENTS

INTRODUCTION

Wayne Gretzky and Sidney Crosby are similar players. But they played in very different eras. When Gretzky was dominating the National Hockey League (NHL) in the 1980s and early '90s, the game was played at a much faster pace. Crosby's NHL today is much more defense oriented.

That makes it difficult to use statistics to compare these players. But it's also not fair to limit a discussion of their greatness to mere numbers. Both legends mean much more to the game than that.

Which one was better? It's an argument without a right or wrong answer. We'll tell their stories and lay out the facts.

GRETZKY OR CROSBY?
YOU DECIDE!

Gretzky shoots against the Calgary Flames.

CHAPTER 1

SHOOTING

Wayne Gretzky fell in love with hockey while growing up in Brantford, Ontario, Canada. He wanted to play every day. But his father grew tired of driving Wayne to the local park to practice. So Walter Gretzky built his son a rink in their back yard. That way Wayne could practice, and Walter could watch from inside the house where it was nice and warm.

It made all the difference for the player known as "The Great One."

All winter long, Wayne would come home from school, throw on skates, grab his stick, and head to the back yard. And the legend of the best player in the history of the game was born.

Gretzky never was the biggest or most powerful player. He made up for it with speed, smarts, and skill. A Wayne Gretzky slap shot or wrist shot didn't blow by the goaltender and rip a hole in the back of

Gretzky didn't have the most powerful shot, but he had plenty of success with it.

the net. He just had a way of putting the puck in the one spot the goalie could not cover.

Wearing his famous No. 99 jersey, Gretzky wasn't shy about taking the puck to the net. "You miss 100 percent of the shots you don't take," he once said.

Gretzky set a single-season record with 92 goals in the 1981–82 season while playing for the Edmonton Oilers. He also shattered another milestone that season. At one time, the NHL played a 50-game schedule. It was a big deal when Maurice Richard scored 50 goals in 50 games for the Montreal Canadiens in 1944–45. Even though the schedule eventually expanded to 80 games, 50 in 50 was still a magic number in hockey. And no NHL player matched that feat until Mike Bossy of the New York Islanders hit the 50/50 mark in 1980–81.

One year later, Gretzky obliterated the record. He scored 50 goals in the Oilers' first 39 games. He set the record by scoring four goals in Game 38 and five more in the next game, a 10–3 victory over the Philadelphia Flyers on December 30, 1981. Those were two of his 10 hat tricks that season, another NHL record.

Gretzky finished his 20-year NHL career with a record 894 goals. Gordie Howe is the only other player in league history to reach the 800-goal mark.

By the time Gretzky retired in 1999, the NHL was changing. The high-scoring days of his prime were long gone. The league's focus had turned to defense. But the league's next offensive-minded star was already preparing to take the NHL by storm.

In Nova Scotia, Canada, a young Sidney Crosby grew up much like Gretzky. Sidney was crazy about hockey from a young age. But there wasn't room in his yard for his father, Troy, to build a practice rink. So the Crosbys used their imagination. They turned part of the basement in their house into a mini-rink. Instead of a goaltender, Sidney would try to shoot the puck into an old clothes dryer.

He would make up games, seeing how many shots it would take for him to score a certain number of goals. He even took advantage of an obstacle in his shooting path. A pole ran from the ceiling to the floor near the dryer. Sometimes, Sidney would try to ding the puck off the pole into the dryer. It helped him practice giving a teammate a chance to deflect the puck on the way to the net.

In his basement, Sidney worked on wrist shots, slap shots, and backhand shots. The dents on the dryer added up over the years. And his hard work paid off when he took the ice.

Compared to the opening in the dryer, a hockey goal must have looked huge.

Sidney could pump in goals quickly, too. While playing major junior hockey for Rimouski Océanic in 2003–04, he scored 66 goals in 62 games.

Crosby has a knack for scoring big goals, such as the gold medal–winner in overtime at the 2010 Olympics.

MEET THE PLAYERS

WAYNE GRETZKY

- Born January 26, 1961, in Brantford, Ontario, Canada
- 6 feet/185 pounds
- Junior teams: Peterborough Petes, 1976–77; Sault Ste. Marie Greyhounds, 1977–78
- Home today: Los Angeles, California

SIDNEY CROSBY

- Born August 7, 1987, in Cole Harbour, Nova Scotia, Canada
- 5 feet, 11 inches/200 pounds
- Junior team: Rimouski Océanic, 2003–05
- Home today: Pittsburgh, Pennsylvania, and Cole Harbour, Nova Scotia

"Sid the Kid" made his NHL debut in 2005 as an 18-year-old for the Pittsburgh Penguins. He was considered the brightest star to come into the league since Gretzky and Penguins owner Mario Lemieux. Crosby more than lived up to the hype.

Like Gretzky, Crosby doesn't have a super-hard shot. He is more focused on putting the puck in the right spot. And he has shown off his scoring touch plenty over the years. Crosby led the league with 52 goals in 2009–10. He won another scoring title with 44 goals in 2016–17, even though he missed the start of the season with a concussion.

Two kids from two different parts of Canada found their own unique ways to get their hockey fix. A backyard rink and a basement dryer helped them make NHL history.

Gretzky keeps his head up, looking for an open teammate at the 1988 NHL All-Star Game.

CHAPTER 2

PASSING

Gretzky and Crosby could fire shots that zipped past goaltenders. But their wizardry on the ice went far beyond just scoring goals. As much as the two superstars liked to shoot, they loved to pass. Their teammates learned to keep their heads up. They never knew when the puck was coming their way.

Gretzky did a lot of work from his "office." That's what he called the space behind the opponent's net. It's a lesson he learned from his dad. Walter Gretzky taught his son to take advantage of the opportunity presented with the play in front of him and with the defenseman and goalie facing the other way.

When young Wayne started taking the puck behind the net, he noticed that when

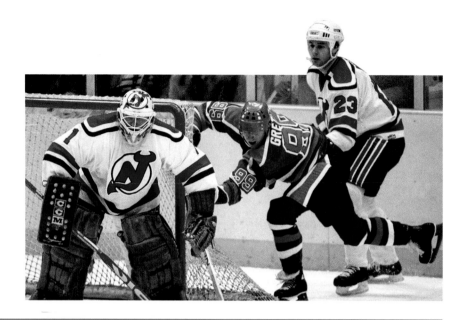

Gretzky did some of his best work from behind the net.

opponents watched him, they couldn't keep an eye on his teammates, too.

"If two guys come at me, then obviously one or two guys are going to be open," Gretzky said.

The "office" was pretty busy during Gretzky's career. His vision and instincts helped him set up easy shots for his teammates. He also was an accurate passer who always seemed to put just the right touch on the puck. That helped him lead the NHL in assists in 16 seasons. No other player has done it more than five times.

His 1,963 career assists are an NHL record, more than 700 assists ahead of Ron Francis, who is second on the all-time list. Gretzky holds the record for most assists in a season with 163 in 1985–86. And he's got the next six highest single-season assist totals in NHL history, too.

Gretzky had the good fortune of playing in the NHL during the 1980s. The league played with a more wide-open style. Goalie equipment was smaller. Scoring totals soared.

By the time Crosby arrived in the league in 2006, the game had changed. Players were bigger and faster. There seemed to be less room on the ice to operate. Teams became better at figuring out how to slow down players who liked to set up in Gretzky's "office."

Of course, that didn't stop Crosby. Like Gretzky, Crosby isn't lightning fast on the ice. But he can see plays before they happen, and he uses his imagination to get his teammates the puck.

When players join the Penguins, they quickly learn to be ready whenever Crosby is on the ice. They never know when he'll find a way to slide a pass onto their stick.

Crosby's passing makes life easier for young linemates such as Conor Sheary, *right*.

Crosby demonstrated that when Pittsburgh won the 2017 Stanley Cup. He had a league-high 19 assists in the playoffs. And he made one of the series-defining plays when the Penguins beat the Nashville Predators in the Stanley Cup Final.

The series was tied at two games apiece. The Penguins were up 3–0 early in the second period of Game 5. Crosby found the puck deep in the Nashville zone. It looked as though he was going to skate behind the net. But instead he slipped a backhand pass that eluded a Predators defenseman and landed on the stick of teammate Conor Sheary, who was alone in front of the net. Sheary jammed the puck into the net to give the Penguins a 4–0 lead. They went on to win the series in six games.

Crosby is one of the top passers in the game.

PROFESSIONAL SUCCESS

WAYNE GRETZKY

- Professional debut: October 14, 1978, with the Indianapolis Racers
- Years active: 1978–99
- 6 Stanley Cup Finals, 4 championships
- All-Star appearances: 18

SIDNEY CROSBY

- Professional debut: October 5, 2005, with the Pittsburgh Penguins
- Years active: 2005–present
- 4 Stanley Cup Finals, 3 championships (through 2017)
- All-Star appearances: 6 (through 2017)

"You can't really draw that up when Sid makes that play," Sheary said.

Crosby's great passing isn't just about his vision. He's pretty tough, too. Crosby isn't huge, but he's strong enough to keep the puck away from opponents. That allows his teammates time to get open.

While Gretzky often had other stars on his line, such as Jari Kurri and Luc Robitaille, Crosby has played with more unproven players. He's always found a way to make them better.

When the Penguins won the 2017 Cup, Crosby played with Sheary and rookie Jake Guentzel. They called the line "Sid and the Kids," because Sheary and Guentzel were 24 and 22 years old, respectively.

Gretzky was a 17-year-old rookie in the final season of the old WHA.

CHAPTER 3

CREATIVITY

Gretzky's coaches gave him a pretty simple order when he was growing up. When they threw the puck on the ice, they told him to "go score."

The coaches didn't care how Gretzky did it. This allowed him to use his imagination. He liked to say that he didn't skate to where the puck was, he was skating to where the puck was going.

Gretzky didn't really have a choice. When he was called up to the professional World Hockey Association (WHA) as a 17-year-old, he was by far the youngest and smallest player on the ice. He needed to use his quickness and his hockey smarts to keep from getting run over.

"Even in the rough-and-tumble WHA when they thought he'd be eaten alive as an 'underage' player, he shined," hockey analyst Tom Tango said.

Gretzky looks for open ice where he can make a play against the Montreal Canadiens.

Gretzky knew most people considered hockey a sport for tough guys. He wanted to show it could be as graceful as ballet, too. He wasn't afraid to try things that other players would not. He usually looked to pass from "the office," but not always.

While playing against the St. Louis Blues in 1981, Gretzky stood behind the net and picked the puck up with his stick. He flicked it off the back of the goalie and watched it drop into the net.

Gretzky's creativity wasn't always just something he came up with on the ice. He spent hours after practice firing at certain spots of the net from different places on the ice. Then at night, he would imagine plays on the ice.

No player made more dreams come true than Gretzky. His play inspired kids across Canada and throughout the world, including a young player learning the game in Cole Harbour, Nova Scotia.

Posters of NHL stars, Gretzky included, lined the wall of Crosby's bedroom. When he was in high school, he liked to watch NHL highlight videos and daydream about making highlight-reel moves of his own.

There are plenty to choose from. Just like Gretzky, Crosby likes to have fun behind the net.

Crosby scored an NHL-high 44 goals during the 2016–17 season. Two came on bank shots off a goaltender's back just like Gretzky used to do. Another came when he shot the puck at New York star goaltender Henrik Lundqvist's face mask on purpose. The puck smacked off Lundqvist's helmet and into the net.

"You don't see that a whole lot," Penguins teammate Bryan Rust said. "At this point, it's not much of a surprise when things like that happen."

Earlier in the same season, Crosby tried to bank the puck off Dallas Stars goaltender Antti Niemi. The puck bounced off

Niemi and came right back to Crosby. So Sid the Kid knocked it out of the air, swinging his stick like a baseball player taking aim at a fastball.

"There aren't too many players in the league that would even think to make that type of play," Penguins coach Mike Sullivan said.

Just like Gretzky before him, Crosby makes them look routine.

Crosby, *left*, finds a creative way to score against Stars goalie Antti Niemi.

IN THE SPOTLIGHT

WAYNE GRETZKY

- Career playoff stats: 122 goals, 260 assists in 208 games

- Career highlight: Gretzky passed Gordie Howe as the NHL's all-time leading goal scorer on March 23, 1994.

- Awards:
  —9 Hart Memorial Trophies (NHL MVP)
  —10 Art Ross Trophies (NHL scoring leader)
  —5 Lady Byng Memorial Trophies (sportsmanship)
  —2 Conn Smythe Trophies (playoff MVP)

- International highlights: With Team Canada, won Canada Cup in 1984, 1987, and 1991; took bronze at the 1978 IIHF World Junior Championships and the 1982 World Championships; took silver at the 1996 World Cup of Hockey

SIDNEY CROSBY

- Career playoff stats: 57 goals, 107 assists in 148 games (through 2017)

- Career highlight: Crosby scored the game-winning goal in the gold-medal game at the 2010 Olympics in Vancouver, British Columbia, Canada.

- Awards:
  —2 Hart Memorial Trophies (NHL MVP)
  —2 Art Ross Trophies (NHL scoring leader)
  —2 Conn Smythe Trophies (playoff MVP)

- International highlights: With Team Canada, won Olympic gold medal in 2010 and 2014; also won 2005 World Junior Championship, 2015 World Championship, and 2016 World Cup of Hockey

The Penguins put the C on Crosby's sweater in 2007.

CHAPTER 4

LEADERSHIP

Being a star in the NHL is a big deal. Being selected as the team captain is an even bigger one. The captain is the leader of the club on the ice and in the locker room. He wears a *C* on his jersey. His jobs include talking to officials during the game and helping teammates when they have a problem.

Of course Gretzky and Crosby were ahead of their time at that, too.

The Penguins made Crosby the youngest captain in NHL history in 2007. He was just 19 years and 297 days old at the time. Pittsburgh actually wanted to make Crosby the captain even earlier. He turned it down. Why? The Penguins were on a hot streak at the time. He didn't want to be selfish and mess things up. Crosby's decision to put the team's needs first was one of the reasons they wanted to make him a captain in the first place.

Even though he was young, it did not take long for the Penguins to follow Crosby's lead. In 2009 the Penguins

Crosby celebrates with the Stanley Cup at a parade in Pittsburgh in June 2017.

won the Stanley Cup. They did it again in 2016 and 2017. While Pittsburgh changed coaches several times during their run, Crosby remained the captain. He made it a point to make sure new players on the team felt welcomed. Whenever a new face joined the club, their lockers were put next to Crosby's. That way Crosby could get to know them and help them feel like they were part of the team.

When 22-year-old Jake Guentzel joined the Penguins in November 2016, Crosby served in his mentor role again. And it paid off. With Crosby's help, Guentzel tied an NHL rookie record with 21 points in the playoffs.

"Growing up, you watch him, so to be honest, it's pretty special," Guentzel said of being Crosby's teammate. "He kind of told me to just play my game."

Crosby's words were important. So were his actions. When the stakes were high, Crosby was at his best. He scored the gold medal–winning goal for Team Canada at the 2010 Winter Olympics. He won the Conn Smythe Trophy as the playoff MVP in both 2016 and 2017, when the Penguins became the first team in nearly 20 years to win back-to-back Stanley Cups.

Just like Crosby, Gretzky was a young captain. The Oilers put the C on his jersey in 1983, when their star forward was just 22 years old. And like Crosby, Gretzky made it a point to put his teammates at ease. While the guys he played with loved winning, they loved the fun of playing with Gretzky even more. Who wouldn't love a guy who feeds you passes right on your blade all night long?

Gretzky put up big numbers in the playoffs, just like he did in the regular season. He is the NHL's all-time leader in playoff points, with 382. Former Edmonton teammate Mark Messier is second with 295.

Gretzky hoists the Stanley Cup with longtime teammate Mark Messier (11).

The number Gretzky was most proud of was the number four. That's how many times Gretzky won the Stanley Cup with the Oilers during the 1980s. The feeling of raising the cup was so special that Gretzky made it his mission to share it with his teammates.

Gretzky also led with his work ethic. Even though he was so talented, he took nothing for granted. His coaches noticed.

"He was always thinking about how to improve himself, the greatest player in the world," said Edmonton coach John Muckler. "I guess that's what made him great. He was always looking for that edge."

An edge no one could match, on or off the ice.

LEGACY

WAYNE GRETZKY

- Important records: NHL's most career points (2,857), goals (894), and assists (1,963); jersey No. 99 retired throughout the NHL; inducted into the Hockey Hall of Fame in 1999

- Key rivals: Mario Lemieux, Brett Hull, Dale Hawerchuck

- Off-ice accomplishments: Started the Wayne Gretzky Foundation, which provides opportunities for children to play hockey; co-authored *99: Gretzky: His Game, His Story*

"It took one practice and one game. I watched him in the morning at the practice and I watched him play that night, and I was convinced that this guy was going to be an incredible player."

—former Oilers coach Glen Sather on how long it took him to realize Gretzky would be great

SIDNEY CROSBY

- Important records: Became youngest NHL captain at age 19 in 2007; joined NHL's 1,000-point club in 2017; third-leading scorer in Pittsburgh Penguins history (through 2016–17 season)

- Key rivals: Alexander Ovechkin, Steven Stamkos

- Off-ice accomplishments: Started the Sidney Crosby Foundation, which brings hockey to disadvantaged children; hosts the Sidney Crosby Hockey School, held every year in his hometown in Nova Scotia

"He's dynamite. He's the best player I've seen since Mario. He's that good."

—Wayne Gretzky

GLOSSARY

ASSIST
A pass or shot that sets up a teammate to score a goal.

BLADE
The part of the stick that handles the puck.

CONCUSSION
The aftereffects of a severe blow to the head.

HAT TRICK
Three goals by the same player in one game.

MILESTONE
An action or event marking a significant change or stage in development.

OVERTIME
An extra period of play when the score is tied after regulation.

RINK
An ice surface on which people skate.

SLAP SHOT
A hard and fast shot with a long backswing and powerful follow-through.

Online Resources

Booklinks
NONFICTION NETWORK
FREE! ONLINE NONFICTION RESOURCES

To learn more about great hockey players, visit abdobooklinks.com. These links are routinely monitored and updated to provide the most current information available.

More Information

Books

Burns, Kylie. *Sidney Crosby*. New York: Crabtree Publishing Company, 2014.

Graves, Will. *The Best Hockey Players of All Time*. Minneapolis, MN: Abdo Publishing, 2015.

Herman, Gail. *Who Is Wayne Gretzky?* New York: Grosset & Dunlap, 2015.

INDEX

ABOUT THE AUTHOR

Will Graves has spent more than two decades as a sportswriter for several newspapers and the Associated Press, covering MLB, the NHL, the NFL, and the Olympics. He's also authored more than a dozen children's sports books. He lives in Pittsburgh, Pennsylvania, with his wife and their two children.